J is for Jesus
An Easter Alphabet and Activity Book

by Debbie Trafton O'Neal

illustrated by Jan Bryan-Hun

For God so loved the world . . .
—D. T. O.

For Amy and Bryan
—J. B. H.

J IS FOR JESUS
An Easter Alphabet and Activity Book

Large-quantity purchases or custom editions of this book are available at a discount
from the publisher. For more information, contact the sales department at Augsburg
Fortress, Publishers, 800-328-4648, or write to: Sales Director, Augsburg Fortress,
Publishers, P. O. Box 1209, Minneapolis, MN 55440-1209.

Book design by Elissa Hudson

ISBN 0-8066-5123-7

The paper used in this publication meets the minimum requirements of American
National Standard for Information Sciences—Permanence of Paper for Printed Library
Materials, ANSI Z329.48-1984.

Manufactured in China.

10   09   08   07   06   1   2   3   4   5   6   7   8   9   10

Dear friends,

I love Easter! Easter is spring days, green grass, chocolate bunnies, and jelly beans. But more importantly, Easter is a reminder of just how much God loves you and me!

This ABC Easter book will help you learn the ABCs, but it is also the story of Holy Week and Easter, the last week that Jesus lived on earth. Choose one or more of your favorite illustrations from the alphabet pages and make some special things to remind you of God's love!

Let this story and these illustrations inspire you to create your own special Easter memories for this year—and for years to come.

Happy Easter!

Debbie Trafton O'Neal

Debbie Trafton O'Neal

As all of the people stood lining the street,

Aa

the children waved branches and
                    danced with their feet.

Bb

Into the crowd, a donkey came through

followed by the disciples,
the friends Jesus knew.

D d

E e

They entered Jerusalem,
after traveling a long way,

joining everyone gathered for the festival day.

Gg

People laid their coats down,
welcoming good news,

singing Hosanna to Jesus,
the King of the Jews.

I i

On Passover evening, they were invited to eat,

and Jesus their friend knelt to wash off their feet.

J j

K k

Jesus taught of God's kingdom,
asking people to care,

and began the Last Supper,
a meal they would share.

Ll

"Remember me," was the message Jesus said. "It is right."

And they ate bread and drank wine
as day turned to night.

"Come with me to the Mountain of Olives," he said. "I know it has been a long day."

The disciples went with him,
but they fell asleep
as Jesus went quietly to pray.

P p

Leaders asked him the question,
"Are you God's Son?"

Jesus replied, "Yes, I am the One."

Ss

"Your sins are forgiven," Jesus said.
"You are free!"

Then he died on a cross
that was carved from a tree.

Tt

Uu

The unmovable moved, the stone rolled away.

Hurray! The first Easter, God's victorious day.

W w

The women ran quickly to find the eleven,

explaining *that* Jesus had gone up to heaven.

And Jesus, the Savior, for me and for you,

is waiting in Zion when this life is through.

Z z

Place mats or Table Runner

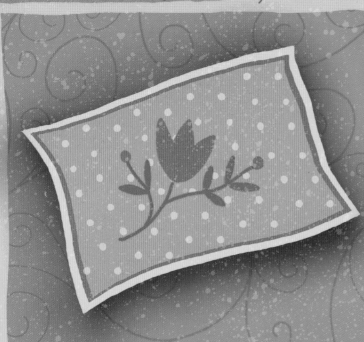

Here's a simple way to make spring table place mats or a table runner! Choose the objects you want and draw them on colorful paper. Cut the shapes out and glue them to a rectangular piece of solid-colored paper, adding a border cut from wrapping paper. Laminate the place mats or table runner with clear laminate film or adhesive paper.

   If you want to make them with fabric, you can use the same method. Cut the shapes from fabric you have stiffened with a sewing adhesive, or use felt. Glue or sew the fabric shapes to a rectangle of colorful print fabric. Add a border if you wish!

Window Paintings

Decorate your windows with springtime Easter designs! Draw simple designs or symbols from the story on white paper. Tape the designs to the outside of your windows with the drawings facing in. Use acrylic, glass or tempera paints to paint your designs on the inside of the window. (Note: Make sure to use paint that you can wash off after Easter!) If you like, outline all of your painting with thin black lines when it is dry. Your windows will look like stained glass!